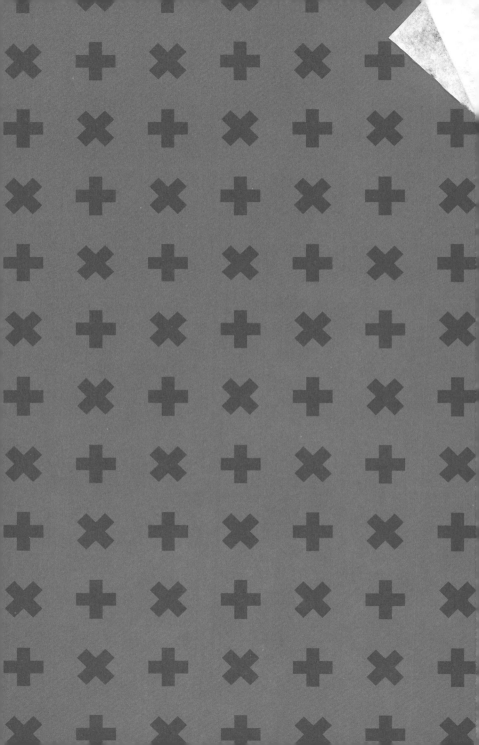

FRONTLINES
AND LIFELINES

COLLECTED POEMS FROM
✦✦✦✦✦ AN ARMY DOCTOR IN ✦✦✦✦✦
CRISIS AND WAR

MAJ. GEN. TIM HODGETTS
CB CBE

✦✦✦✦✦✦✦✦✦✦✦✦✦✦✦✦✦✦✦✦✦✦✦✦✦

FOREWORD BY
FRANK GARDNER

✦✦✦✦✦✦✦✦✦✦✦✦✦✦✦✦✦✦✦✦✦✦✦✦✦

Published in 2024 by Unicorn
an imprint of Unicorn Publishing Group
Charleston Suite, Meadow Business Centre
Lewes, East Sussex
BN8 5RW
www.unicornpublishing.org

10 9 8 7 6 5 4 3 2 1

ISBN 978-1-916846-31-9

Design by Matthew Wilson
Printed by Gutenberg Press, Malta

Cover image:
The Surgeon's Boots
© Gordon Rushmer (Art.IWM ART 18036),
reproduced with permission.

This image is of Tim Hodgetts' boots soiled with
blood and was painted to represent the poem *Dressing
the Dead*. The painting is part of the Imperial War
Museum collection.

To Mags and Jack

*with royalties donated in support of
The Poppy Factory registered charity*

CONTENTS

....

FOREWORD

WARS END, BUT NOT FOR EVERYONE. THERE ARE FEW PEOPLE better qualified than Gen Hodgetts to remind us that for those who have come through them, often outwardly unscathed, the hidden scars remain, long after the conflict has ended.

The first time I heard his poetry – I think it was 'Major Incident!' – I was moved to tears. It was not just the power of his poetry, it was a reminder of the terrible choices thrust onto the shoulders of trauma medics, especially in a theatre of war: that grim prioritisation of the likely-to-live over the likely-to-die.

This resonated for me. After being shot six times in a terrorist attack in Saudi Arabia my life hung in the balance. By the time the trauma team reached me my core body temperature had dropped to 30C. I had gone into something known as 'Disseminated Intravascular Coagulation', or 'DIC', also known grimly in the trade as 'Death Is Coming'. I was bleeding uncontrollably from 11 bullet holes. As fast as they poured blood in, out it came through the holes, like filling up a bath without a plug. Close to giving up, the surgeons tried a certain clotting agent and it worked. But it could so easily have gone the other way.

Gen Tim's poems resonate in another way too. Flying back from Kandahar after reporting on Op Moshtarek in 2010, I found myself in the front of the RAF plane while next to me a team of medics worked tirelessly on a soldier who had lost both his legs to an IED. He was heavily sedated yet I knew that when he came round in a Birmingham hospital he would be suddenly confronted with the unwelcome sight of his new body. His first reaction would probably be 'where's the rest of my platoon?' But 21st century medicine has advanced so much that, thanks to those medics, and to those who treated him back at Camp

Bastion, his life was saved and he had a chance of starting over with a set of prosthetic legs.

Gen Tim's poems are a testimony to so much that we don't always see on the News about the wars of our time: the intimate detail, the poignant observations, the black humour of the squaddie that can poke fun at a situation in even the darkest of hours.

This is an important work and it is a privilege to have been asked to write this Foreword.

Frank Gardner

PREFACE

....

THIS WORK REFLECTS MY PERSONAL EXPERIENCE OF CONFLICT, crisis, and war, from Northern Ireland in the early 1990s, through the Kosovo, Iraq, and Afghanistan campaigns, to the Covid-19 pandemic and the Russo–Ukraine war. A few poems have been published previously. Many have been shared with the public in museum exhibitions or public readings, often raising funds for military-related charities. Others have had no prior exposure.

In poetry I have found the ability to say what is otherwise difficult or unpalatable. Some of the poems are critical and challenging; some are humorous, as dark humour is a well-recognised tool of the resilient soldier. All are observational and grounded in the realities of crisis, conflict, and the environment of war. You will also find deep remembrance. What they share is that they represent lived experience; and all have provided catharsis in their writing.

I have used rhyme as a tool for education throughout my medical career, starting with the publication of Rhythms in Rhyme in the British Association for Immediate Care Journal, 1993:[1]

> *Two-hundred, two-hundred, three-sixty, then*
> *Tube,[2] IV,[3] adrenaline,*
> *Two minutes CPR, and then*
> *Three-sixty thrice and round again.[4]*

Twenty-five years later I returned to the four-line stanza to teach principles of catastrophic bleeding control to the public in the event of a deliberate terrorist attack, and to overcome half a century of first aid dogma that precluded using a tourniquet for life-threatening limb bleeding (when the alternative is to watch a patient die):

If I've tried to pack and press,
Or there is no other way
To stop the bleeding, more or less,
I can use a tourniquet!

This tourniquet rule features in materials of *citizenAID*, a charity[5] that I co-founded in 2017. It distributes educational materials to schools that offer primary-aged children guidance on how to stay safe, with song lyrics written to the tunes of *London's Burning* and *Three Blind Mice*.

Yet the reason I started writing poetry in earnest was as a means of reflecting on traumatic or morally injurious experiences from the Second Gulf War, in 2003, and through subsequent tours; four of Iraq and three of Afghanistan. Writing has often felt pressing within days of the experience. Why? Because how else to defuse as the medical director and senior doctor in a persistently stressed field hospital? In this setting colleagues and junior staff are looking to you for leadership, support, and strength in moral adversity. How else to compartmentalise what you have experienced: the unprecedented, unimaginable, and macabre? It becomes critical to find an effective way to mentally reset for the next patient or challenge.

The concept of moral injury came to the fore during the Covid-19 pandemic. Civilian clinicians were forced into decisions they had never previously entertained: patients had to be prioritised on expected outcome (predicted by age and comorbidity) or on the availability of ventilator beds, rather than on strict clinical need. Overstretched staffing ratios meant the high quality care that doctors and nurses wanted to deliver was unachievable.

"Welcome to the world of military medicine!" I would say: with casualty bursts exceeding available resources, and a fragile contested supply chain that is thousands of miles long, military clinicians are used to difficult choices. We expect to be placed in morally injurious situations. Nevertheless, some situations cannot be adequately imagined or fully prepared for, and we have been conditioned to respond unemotionally. My poems draw on those experiences and offer personal insight into the ever-present moral jeopardy of the conflict environment.

What do I hope to achieve in bringing them into public view? Likely, you have read war poetry from the soldier's perspective, but have you previously encountered the viewpoint of those who manage the consequences of war? I am revealing this alternative perspective. My poems are not anti-war. I believe war to be an inevitable necessity that meets political ends when national interests remain threatened and where diplomacy has failed. But decisions towards war must always be cognisant of the human consequences. We remember those who give their lives, endure life-changing injuries, or suffer the mental ill-health consequences of what they have seen and done in contact with the enemy; but let us also remember that saving lives in conflict, picking up those human pieces, takes a parallel toll on the carers.

In Afghanistan over the hectic summer of 2009, leading a multinational field hospital as the deployed medical director, I was asked by BBC Radio 4 to pre-record some of this poetry for Remembrance Day. I made my selection and submitted them for clearance, but was authorised to recite only a single verse from a single poem. At that time, the remainder was deemed "too sensitive" to release into the public domain.

Fifteen years on, I hope the world is now receptive to my work, and that it is acceptable to air without being considered sensational. Yes, the topics of ethics, dying and death can be difficult – even uncomfortable – and maybe certain poems should come with a health warning. After all, even a weekday television soap opera is prefixed by an announcement that the episode may cause offence. But please remember that this all happened. It is purely observational. If you are affected by anything you read, talk to someone. If you are not affected, you might want to check your pulse.

Major General Tim Hodgetts
CB CBE KHS OStJ DL
Birmingham 2024

INTRODUCTION

WAR AND CONFLICT HAVE BEEN RECURRING THEMES IN POETRY throughout history from Ancient Greece and Homer's *Iliad* through to notable First World War poets Wilfred Owen, Siegfried Sassoon, or Rupert Brooke; and Hodgetts' work becomes the latest addition to the pantheon of works within this genre. War poetry emerged as a powerful expression of the human experience of conflict that articulates the harsh realities of war and explores themes such as the futility of war, the loss of innocence, the psychological trauma endured by soldiers, and the broader societal implications of armed conflict. Many poets draw on personal experiences, vivid imagery, and poignant language to capture the devastating effects of war on both the soldiers on the front lines and the civilians caught in its wake. Through their verses, war poets provide a unique and empathetic view into the human condition during times of strife, offering readers a profound insight into the consequences of war.

Before discussing Hodgetts' work in detail, it is important to consider its home within the medical humanities – a field that blends the expertise of healthcare with the insights of the humanities, providing a unique lens through which to explore the human dimensions of medicine. Within this rich tapestry, poetry emerges as a poignant and evocative medium, allowing for a profound exploration of the emotional, ethical, and cultural aspects of health, harm, and healing. One compelling facet of this intersection is the exploration of army doctors' experiences through the lens of poetry.

The life of an army doctor is marked by the dual roles of healer and witness to the human toll of conflict. Hodgetts' poetry becomes a vehicle through which he can articulate the complexities of his experiences, delving into emotional landscapes shaped by the trauma of war, resilience of the human spirit, and the ethical dilemmas inherent in his roles. These verses offer a window into the unique challenges faced by those who navigate the intersection of medicine and the military, capturing the visceral realities and profound moments that defined his service. Through the medium of poetry, Hodgetts' narratives contribute to the broader dialogue within medical humanities, shedding light on the sacrifices, triumphs, and moral reflections that accompany the practice of medicine in the challenging context of armed conflict. In so doing, this exploration not only deepens our understanding of the human experience in times of war but also underlines the crucial role of the arts in fostering empathy, resilience, and a more inclusive comprehension of the profound connections between health, humanity, and the military experience.

In L.P. Hartley's novel *The Go-Between*, the renowned opening line, "The past is a foreign country; they do things differently there," serves as a contemplation on the essence of the past, memory, and the influence of time on human existence. This suggests that the past exists as a distinct realm from the present, and is characterised by its own traditions, values, and ways of life. Describing the past as a foreign country conveys a sense of otherness and unfamiliarity. Additionally, the statement "they do things differently there" underscores the cultural and societal disparities across different time periods. It implies that the customs, norms, and attitudes of the past may diverge from contemporary sensibilities.

Recollection is more than keeping people and events alive in awareness, it means crafting an existence for these memories and allowing them to mature on paper. Through this process of remembering and creating, Hodgetts came to embrace his identity as a poet. He opens our eyes to the fact that war poetry has at its heart the ultimate responsibility to tell the truth. An undisputable honesty lies in the creation of much of the work presented in this book. It recalls over 35 years history of witnessing the very worst outcomes of war, the gruelling choices to be made of life and death, the mending and reconstructing of bodies and the realisation that a red cross – rather than a protection – becomes the best of targets for the enemy to undermine morale. In his poetry, we are immersed in the experiences of a soldier and doctor within the context of modern conflict, exploring themes of politics, environment of war, death and dying, and remembrance. Many of these themes highlight a strangely familiar connection with the past and the poetry of the First World War.

The journey begins with *Belfast Bomb*, a poem from 1991, which recounts the IRA bomb that deliberately targeted hospital staff while they were watching the England vs Australia rugby match. This is perhaps one of the longest poems in the book leaving the reader in no doubt that the casualties were *'Its doctors, nurses, children, / who are the injured trapped and dead'*. This experience clearly marked the beginning of a lifelong journey of remembrance for Hodgetts, but this reminiscence also influences his narrative style by becoming an overt physical presence in his poems, not just by being the future promise of what is presently being read, but by almost becoming another character in the work.

When he writes of his memory, he compares it to the countless victims of many wars he has witnessed. Through constant reminder of the horrors of war, its outcomes, and personification, Hodgetts creates an energy that haunts the reader but is also a familiar entity that must be salvaged. Such realisation was also evident in First World War poetry where the words of highly educated young men used poetry and prose to create a picture of the horrors of what lay before them in war. Hodgetts joins the ranks of such war poets using personal narrative voices in their desire to connect with a larger community. This invites readers to contemplate the dynamic interplay between time, memory, and the ever-evolving landscape of human experience. Upon reflection, it raises the possibility that the past might not be as "foreign" as initially perceived.

In Owen's *Dulce et Decorum Est*, he narrates a gas attack experience. Nearly a century later, Hodgetts' *Chemical Alarm* highlights the uncanny familiarity of the past. Both works depict the urgent warning "Gas!", the frantic efforts to don protective masks and suits, bridging the temporal gap with shared experiences of chaos during a gas attack. Where the pieces differ is in their respective endings. Hodgetts' experience was a false alarm, whereas Owen would witness the harrowing death of a man: '*And watch the white eyes writhing in his face, / His hanging face, like a devil's sick of sin; / if you could hear at every jolt, the blood / Come gargling from the froth-corrupted lungs*'.

This is not to say that such graphic accounts are not evident in the work of Hodgetts: in *Rose Cottage* and *The Extra Leg*, he creates a truly unforgettable story, with such direct opening lines that accentuate memory and make it clear that reflecting and recalling are important not just for him but also for the victim and the family left bereft. As he describes the silence he encounters, he clearly wants to capture the universality of this state, thereby directly challenging the reader to comprehend the horror. He describes '*I'm looking at a bag of parts, / A booted leg is out of place; / We've matched most limbs to chests and guts / And heads without a face*', as you can imagine, if you allow yourself to visualise such gruesomeness, the entire image becomes so graphic that it explains the need to sometimes be silenced by fear. Remembering is so important to him that he speaks of a divine mission, inspired by the spirits, and recounted through the hymn that he hears in his head. This need to remember is a force that will not let go, and so becomes a duty to recall through *A Hymn for Helmand*.

Paradox of the Injured sees Hodgetts question injury itself in its many forms and the meaning it may have for the footballer who fears '*he has lost his career; / While the soldier now has hope to bear*', because – despite the pain and injury – it may be his ticket home. In ***Balls, Ethical Choices***, and ***Amputee*** he moves on to focus on the outcomes of his medical interventions and questions the efficacy of his actions; although a life might be saved, the quality of life for the survivor could be debatable. This reflection brings into focus the point that those returning from war are forever changed, and Sassoon shares similar sentiments in his poem ***They:*** *"'We're none of us the same!" the boys reply. / "For George lost both his legs; and Bill's stone blind; / Poor Jim's shot through the lungs and like to die; / And Bert's gone syphilitic: you'll not find / A chap who's served that hasn't found some change.'"* In Hodgetts ***Amputee*** and Owen's ***Disabled***, we see the impact of injury – specifically the loss of limbs – as a central theme. They also touch on how these injuries might impair perceptions of masculinity, their ability to work, self-sufficiency or their chance to find love.

While most poems focus on loss, they do so in a broader manner, often employing techniques of magical pragmatism to express the effects of upheaval and the need to find a home. At certain points in the work, we see how Hodgetts introduces variations of structure and style of poetry that create a constant shift of focus, yet their essence is the same. In ***Ghosts of Normandy***, we are acquainted with several perspectives of the same place through the ghostly eyes of both antagonist and defender. Through the eyes of a doctor, ***The Best Team*** and ***The Combat Medic's Countdown*** deliver a factual yet harrowing account of the assessment, treatment, and fight to keep people alive; the reliance on skills; and the fight against the greatest nemesis, time. Interestingly, in ***Flag of Remembrance*** and ***Balls***, Hodgetts may unwittingly pay homage to Guillaume Apollinaire, who served as an infantry officer in the First World War and wrote *Calligrammes – poems of peace and war* (1913–16). The words of these poems are spatially arranged to create an image while also representing a form of free writing, where ideas are not necessarily expressed in verse: they do not have a recognised rhyming pattern and rather serve to provide an iconic image that can express more than the words alone.

Before he recounts his deployments, Hodgetts already shows a glimpse of what he gained from his experience. He notes that it is this constant remembering that leads to his creation of the poems in the first place. Indeed, so much memory seeks release after his return from each conflict that remembering and creating accumulate to form the script. In other words, the poems in which he is a character are also the product of his deployments. This book of poems is a physical monument to memory, ethical choices, feelings of loss and pain, and – for him – both the completion of his missions, and the beginning of a new completeness. To form this testament to memory and to sing the silenced words of known hymns, he chooses to stress recall, not only through *what* is said but also through *how* it is said.

Throughout his journey, Hodgetts recognises that it is not enough to recollect his patients, but that he must adopt the identity of the poet and set their memories to paper and song. In this role, he aims for the ultimate: the battle to capture the reality of his past and to conserve these experiences through his articulation of words and music. In so doing, he must overcome the prevailing culture of silence — a silence that exists not only in war and medicine but also threatens in the homeland. In the poems *You're Going To War So Worry*, *Ramp Ceremony*, *COVID Funeral and COVID P.P.E.*, we see Hodgetts is unsilenced while exploring themes of propaganda, betrayal, the hypocrisy in politics, and the ineptitude to effectively supply the frontline, whether that be those deployed in a theatre of war or those on the wards of a hospital – making life itself expendable. This is not too dissimilar from Sassoon's poem *Base Details*, in which he provides a contemptuous portrayal of those who benefit from war but do not experience its horrors firsthand: '*and when the war is done and youth stone dead, / I'd toddle safely home and die – in a bed*'.

In these poems, experience and memory shape narrative forms and strategies toward reclaiming a suppressed past and help the process of re-visioning what is essential to gaining control over one's life and future. In *Bagram Belly*, *Field Dining*, *COVID Funeral*, and *COVID P.P.E.*, we witness a very different type of conflict: a war on disease. This unseen enemy can be just as deadly as the injuries sustained in open conflict. Here, too, we see the personal loss of a father during a fight with the unseen enemy Covid-19. The annals of history are peppered with failure of military campaigns due to the spread of pestilence and disease. Finally, in another of Hodgetts' poems *In memoriam of Dr Ross*, he commemorates the first woman in Scotland to gain a medical degree, who subsequently died of typhus while tending to Serbian victims of the typhus epidemic during the First World War.

In this 35-year journey – and despite his training as a doctor and a soldier – Hodgetts gains a new identity as a poet through his expression of words and memory. This was, perhaps, a part of himself that was always there, trapped like his memories, and through this releases that which was buried even deeper – his human identity. And so, he shows that the poet must combine his military and medical self to become whole and presents a sequence of different paths that are all a part of the culture of war, blending past heritage with present concerns and thereby forging the way for a new, mixed future. His poems, then, are textually important to him, as a creator of war poetry heritage, and now also to become part of the continuation of such literature. Despite the arguments over literature regarding war and the outcomes of war, and the debate over what can be considered a truly clear description of this, Hodgetts manages to capture the confusion of it all and – through this recollection of his journey – creates a mix of narratives, memories, events, and people that symbolise the blend that encompasses the experience of war in all its facets.

Professor Gerri Matthews-Smith
Director for Military Research
Education & Public Engagement

Ian S H Sudlow-McKay
Heritage Collections Manager
War Poets Collection, Craiglockhart

Edinburgh Napier University, March 2024

ORIGINS

BELFAST BOMB

In 1991 I was posted to Northern Ireland as resident physician for the Military Wing of Musgrave Park Hospital, Belfast. I was on duty on 2 November, at 3.53 p.m. when an IRA bomb exploded. It had targeted hospital staff watching the England vs Australia Rugby World Cup final in the basement social club. I took charge, as senior clinician present (although the junior officer), and assumed the role of Medical Commander to evacuate the hospital and set up an improvised casualty clearing centre in the road. This event has had a profound effect on my career to champion developing civilian and military international standards to manage the scene of a multiple casualty incident. This poem is therefore an 'origins' story: it has provided over thirty years of enduring motivation.

Belfast, I've been often told,
Is beautiful to see,
But murdered friends, near-death escaped,
Colour my memory.

November 1991:
The 'World in Union',[6]
Fans crowded into Twickenham,[7]
English Lions poised to win.

In Belfast, at the hospital
That housed a military wing,
Soldiers gathered in the social club
To hear their heroes sing.

The night before I'd had a drink
To mark my end of tour,
I didn't pause at all to think
My life would change this hour.

It was quite serendipitous,
The doctors watched them play
In the comfort of the officers' mess
Three hundred yards away.

At near full-time the windows shook
Before the *THUMP* was heard.
I stood to see a pall of smoke:
Could this be what we'd feared?

"Was that a bomb?" I asked out loud,
And grabbed my stethoscope.
I ran out past the sergeants' mess
And mustered staff to cope.

Our mess was in a small compound,
Protected by a fence.
Running towards the hospital
The silence was intense.

In tunnel underneath the road,
A bomb against the fire door
Like cannon blast, had caused collapse
Of first onto the ground floor.

I was not quite the first on scene –
Our chef was just ahead;
I left him be to dig through bricks,
No words needed be said.

The operating theatre
Was now open to the air,
Smoke rising through the rubble
From the basement spreading fire.

Although just a young captain,
I was the best man trained
To react in a disaster,
With the exams I'd gained.[8]

The medic on reception
Was shocked and paralysed,
But responded to direction,
And got help mobilised.

My first concern was patients
Already on the wards;
To get them all to safety
I had to break down doors.

The A&E[9] was destroyed,
The situation dire,
Without the kit we could not hope
To give our patients care.

Where could we treat the injured?
We had to improvise.
I took a friend to I.T.U[10]
To scavenge some supplies.

Out on the road we gathered,
And organised ourselves
In makeshift teams, and waited
For rescue of our friends.

Adjacent to the soldiers
Was a ward for sick children;
The windows had been blown out
But no harm had come to them.

Belfast's biggest ever response
Was to a call that said,
"It's doctors, nurses, children,
Who are the injured, trapped, and dead".

Five hours slipped by so quickly
As the rescue carried on,
Before I thought to ring home
Through my quarter's military phone.[11]

The news had been reporting
That the bomb was in the Mess.
False conclusions had been drawn –
I found the priest at my address.[12]

I unpacked all my boxes
And sat up all the night,
Recording all I'd seen and done,
To get the story right.

I left as planned at first light,
Pain on my driver's face,
One of the dead was his friend:
He'd experienced God's grace.

On the plane I saw the papers,
As if from another world,
From this complex situation,
Without debrief, I'd been hurled.

I thought I'd be contacted,
Having led the on-scene care;
No word meant I suspected
They'd forgotten I was there.

For some time I was angry,
Yet this motivated me
To mitigate disasters
Where preparedness is key.

I dedicate this poem
To those who lost their lives.[13]
They have been my inspiration,
Silent champions in my eyes.

CLINICAL
CHALLENGE

THE COMBAT MEDIC'S COUNTDOWN

COMBAT MEDICAL TECHNICIANS ARE THE ARMY'S MEDICS AND paramedics. They work independently on foot patrol or in an ambulance. Trained in advanced resuscitation skills, they form part of the doctor-led team in regimental aid posts, on helicopters or in field hospitals. This poem featured in the National Army Museum's 2013 *Unseen Enemy* exhibition, London.

10 minutes until help arrives,[14]
To assess, treat and keep alive.

9-liner[15] tells the HQ where
To send the chopper and with what gear.

8 are the eyes that scan each move:
The medic's skills to them must prove.

7-inches wide, the ragged wound,
He packs with gauze and shrimp shells ground.[16]

6 ribs he carefully counts down,
(The drain's landmark for lung that's blown).[17]

5-hundred mls saline ensures
The boost to falling blood pressure.[18]

4 attempts to find a vein
To give the drugs to relieve pain.

3 too many in my view!
(I.O.'s easy to push fluids through).[19]

2 tourniquets, applied each side,
To stop the bleeding from both thighs.

1 medic to do all of this.
You may agree – it takes the piss.

"MAJOR INCIDENT!"

A MAJOR INCIDENT IS DECLARED WHEN IMMEDIATELY AVAILABLE resources are overwhelmed by surging casualty numbers. This results in off-duty or sleeping staff being called urgently to assist. As the staff numbers in a field hospital are relatively small, and bursts of critical casualties common, a major incident is experienced much more often than in civilian hospitals. As a professor of Emergency Medicine and a co-author of the international MIMMS system to manage mass casualties (*Major Incident Medical Management and Support*) – such incidents were my bread and butter.

> *"It's major incident stand-by!"*
> Warns us brown stuff's about to fly.
> No casualties are yet confirmed,
> Crash details we have not yet learned,
> An 'aircraft down' is all we know,
> Not when, how many, where or how.
>
> The senior staff then all stand-to,
> Calm down the young, put on a brew,
> Exude an air of confidence
> Born from repeat experience,
> Plan for the worst scenario,
> Sketch pictures of the casualty flow.

"It's major incident declared!"
We've half an hour left to prepare,
A tannoy message reaches all
On duty in the hospital,
The trauma team needs paging too
(Could be at lunch or in the loo).

Prep resus bays, wipe clean the board,
Get current patients to the ward,
Draw up the drugs, demand 'shock packs',[20]
Lay down the law to embed hacks,[21]
Ensure all staff wear PPE,[22]
And use the time for nervous wee.

"Wheels up at scene!",[23] they'll soon be here,
All teams stand poised, no hint of fear;
Bays improvised in outside shade
(Required capacity's been made)
Fill like a diastolic heart[24]
With bodies from Larrey's new cart.[25]

First to arrive has inhaled smoke
(Airway oedema makes him choke),[26]
Coughing up phlegm and thick black soot,
His skin is burned from head to foot –
With the exception of his soles,
And panicked eyes in leathered holes.

Though he's awake he'll surely die;
No tears from him, he cannot cry.
The staff exchange a knowing glance,
The signs are clear: he's got no chance,
A bay is free, label T4,[27]
I estimate two hours, no more.

More injured come, we're soon full up,
All teams flat out and stretched to cope,
A slick conveyor belt of care,
Consultant judging that all's fair,
Resources mean 'do best for most',
The Gandhi ideal has been lost.[28]

"It's major incident stand down!"
No injured left to treat remain.
We look for beer, our thoughts to drown,
In uniform with dried blood stains.

The inner stain we can't wash clean,
A lasting print of the events
Shapes life, career, and self-esteem,
After a *major incident*.

SANGIN VALLEY

In 2007, the Sangin Valley in Helmand Province, Afghanistan, was notorious for the level of Taliban insurgent activity and high number of British casualties. The Medical Emergency Response Team (MERT) provided immediate advanced treatment for the injured during flight to the field hospital in a Chinook helicopter. That year, I did a tour as a Consultant Emergency Medicine and MERT doctor.

Fifty feet above the ground,
Spewing seven-point-six-two lead,[29]
Banks to fool a MANPAD firer:[30]
Bullets split the Taliban's head.[31]

RPG,[32] nine-hundred yards,
The safety fuse will make charge blow,
Good job it is bloody hard
Predicting where the chopper goes.

SAM locked-on: cock-pit alarm,[33]
Chaff and flares burst out her tail.
Turns and dives to avoid harm,
Helpless freight looks sick and pale.

Higher up, two-thousand feet,
Apache[34] views the threat on ground:
Hellfire[35] sends the beard to meet
Allah, with an explosive sound.

Screaming up the Sangin valley,
Twin rotors drag the heavy bird.
Small rounds chase the flight in vollies,
Each Kevlar 'ping' by aircrew heard.[36]

The landing zone's a poppy field,
Brown scored heads in down-draft sway.
A paradox that this crop's yield
Could take our soldiers' pain away.

Enemy fire strafes the aircraft,
The Quick Reaction Force deploys.
Mini-gun puffs its metal hatred,[37]
Our patients' pleas are drowned in noise.

As if on a giant bungee,
We lurch again into the sky.
On our knees we offer comfort
To limbless comrades as they die.

Oil pressure is reducing;
Hydraulic system has been hit.
No 'comms'[38] for medics means that nothing
Is known of a potential ditch.

Chinook returns to Bastion:[39]
Human cargo sighs relief.
A little battle has been won –
Some relatives denied their grief.

THE BEST TEAM

A HIGH PERFORMING RESUSCITATION TEAM, OR TRAUMA TEAM, is often compared to a *Formula 1* pit crew. Everyone knows their task; one they complete in a high-pressure environment with little or no instruction. The team leader watches closely for any deviation or unexpected occurrence, at which point they step in to correct or control the team. This poem has two voices – of the pit crew and of the trauma team

PIT CREW	TRAUMA TEAM
"I've got a puncture	
On the rear right.	
I'm losing traction –	
The steering feels tight."	
	"His left lung's been punctured,
	Stabbed twice in a fight.
	He's losing blood pressure –
	Says his chest feels tight."
Protected and ready,	
The pit team is coiled	
As the spring in a rifle,	
Cleaned, cocked and oiled.	
	Dispersed team members
	Doing rounds, drinking tea,
	Respond to the fast bleep,
	"TRAUMA TEAM – A and E!"[40]

No words are needed,
So practiced are they,
Each has their position
In the pit bay.

Competitive doctors,
Who all want to heal,
Vie for position –
Their turn at the wheel.

Ten seconds of action,
Unflappable manner.
Tyres off and replaced
With pneumatic spanner.

Team orders are given
From foot of the bed.
Gasman[41] with drugs
Is poised at the head.

With a wheel spin he's off
To rejoin the track;
The champion driver,
Chequered flag at his back.

Eyelids flutter – he's off
To sleep while they try
To win against odds
That all logic defies.

BAGRAM BELLY

THE TWENTY-FIRST CENTURY CAMPAIGN IN AFGHANISTAN
from late 2001, initially involved British troops working out of
Bagram, a disused Soviet airbase from their Afghan war, 1979–1989.
I was deployed to Bagram in 2002, at short notice, to improve the
base's medical plan, then got stuck in the field hospital when the
incumbent emergency consultant became ill. Days later, a mystery
infectious disease swept through the hospital staff, leading to crisis as
the hospital began to fail, at which point I (as a professor of emergency
medicine) took charge…

"The MEDPLAN's a turd, go polish a turd!"[42]
The instruction was given to me.
No training was needed (it seems absurd);
I flew out to Kabul[43] that week.

The hospital sat on a disused airbase,
In mountainous foothills near Bagram.
Ordnance was bulldozed aside in great haste
(Left over from Russian invasion).

I expected to stay only four or five days
And had foolishly packed a light bag.
Reflecting, this was the viral growth phase,
Behind which contagion will lag.

My colleague got sick and he was flown home;
I now was in charge of the E.D.
The following day they started to come,
Meningitis, puking, and L.O.C.[44]

On day three I wrote (I kept a strict log)
"Like Chard at Rorke's Drift".[45] I was standing
Amongst fallen friends, in clinical fog,
With no clear diagnosis forthcoming.

Sixty per cent of the hospital staff
Were so sick they were unfit for duty.
Quarantined (guards blocking every path),
We sought help from a neighbouring country.

From our military base in southern Oman,[46]
A team was assembled and briefed:
"It's an unknown disease – every man[47]
Is at risk – this is Op Certain Death".

The specialist nurses were the worst hit,
(From treating the most severe cases).
The virus passed on through vomit and shit
Aerosolised on their faces.

To protect the well I gave them all pills,
Tracing who the sick were contacting.
To cover the staff gaps left by the ill,
In five different roles I was acting.

The Rad Tech[48] I thought had a critical task –
He was ordered to stay in his tent.
If urgently needed he'd wear his gas mask
To X-ray those tubed on a vent.[49]

I found out the value of 'telemedicine',[50]
Which simply meant use of the phone
(Not email or broadband with images in)
To call experts and colleagues at home.

An infectious cause was abundantly clear
And so was the D.S solution:[51]
Stringent hand-washing and protective wear –
The solution to pollution's dilution.[52]

The first patient flown back by UK C-CAST[53]
Passed the bug on to all of the crew,
Whose mystery illness admitted them fast
(Bio-warfare had dawned on a few).[54]

On Bagram the hospital ran out of drugs,
Cefotaxime[55] the notable one,
The antibiotic 'to kill all known bugs';
A replacement was needed at once.

The German field hospital based in Kabul
Sent a drug with a similar range;
The French helped with much needed plasma in bottles,[56]
While American friends found us planes.

At ten days we finally got a break through,
Announced on the BBC World Service:
Electron microscopy[57] of patients' poo
Had identified a norovirus.[58]

Surprised but relieved, we had contained the spread
And defeated this new viral strain.
Some thoughtless, inaccurate things had been said
By those looking to apportion blame.

In the myths of the Corps this is 'Bagram Belly',
An unfortunate spate of the runs,
Which weakens the lessons for history,
For the sake of alliterative pun.

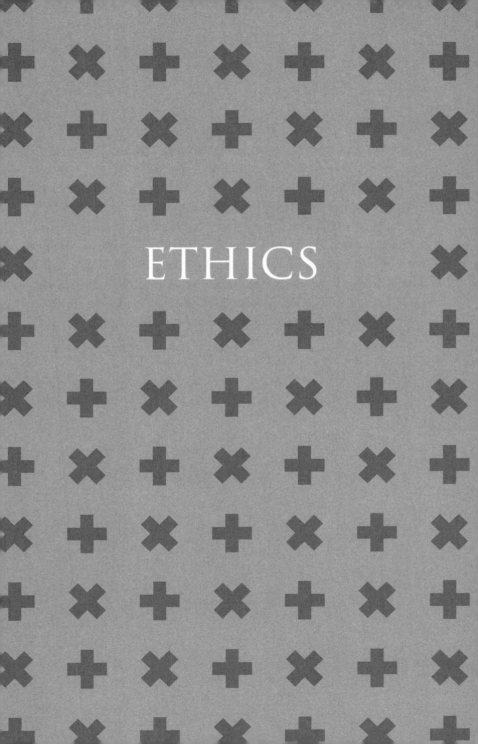

ETHICS

A DOCTOR OR A SOLDIER FIRST?

MEDICAL PERSONNEL, VEHICLES AND TREATMENT FACILITIES are protected from attack during armed conflict by the Geneva Convention. They are identified by a Red Cross, or related emblem (Red Crescent or Red Crystal). Yet, throughout contemporary history, belligerents have frequently ignored this protection and deliberately targeted medical capabilities to undermine their opponents' morale. This breaches both the Law of Armed Conflict and International Humanitarian Law, but has been witnessed at scale in the Russian war against Ukraine since February 2022. This poem captures the resulting ethical tension for military doctors under deliberate attack.

"A *doctor* or a soldier first?"
A common ask by those unversed
In risks they cannot understand,
Nor visualise; like glove on hand
Sits medicine on soldiering.

For in dilemma floundering,
Young doctors in a firefight choose
Between their oath[59] or life to lose,
While Red Cross armbands have become
A target for the sniper's gun.
Conventions from Geneva hold,
A unilateral moral code.

"A *soldier* or a doctor first?"
My wounded ethics can be nursed;
It's preferable than my brains spilled
On poppies in an Afghan field.

ETHICAL CHOICES

ETHICAL CHOICES WAS WRITTEN TO REFLECT ON THE DAILY
ethical challenges I faced as medical director of the British field
hospital in Afghanistan, 2009. There were no right or wrong answers,
only exquisitely difficult choices, every day, about the lives of the
critically wounded.

1

Admit: don't admit?
There's one bed left. An injured child
Fell down a well,
Is very sick,
But there's a TIC.[60]
I feel compelled,
For soldiers' sake, to hold that bed.
Admit: don't admit?

2

Treat: don't treat?
He's got no legs, his heart has stopped,
Stood on a mine,
Will likely die,
But shall I try?
Two out of nine
Will get pulse back; we've changed the odds.
Treat: don't treat?

3

Live: or let die?
We've tried for hours, he won't respond;
Fresh donor blood
Was our last card.
Though it is hard
I won't, but could
Lack courage, not accept the end.
Live: or let die?

SNIFFER DOGS

AT CAMP BASTION IN AFGHANISTAN THE OFFICER COMMANDING the working dogs' pound allowed senior field hospital doctors to take the sniffer dogs for their daily afternoon walk. For a dog lover this was a welcome relief.

On more than one occasion a working dog was rushed to the field hospital for treatment, when injured or sick with heat stroke. Yet doctors are not licensed to treat animals...

It's been a long day at the office,
Where can relaxation be found?
In the friendship with no strings or malice,
From the dogs in the working dogs' pound.

There are two types of dog and they differ –
There is one type you *don't* want to stroke –
The Labs and the Spaniels are sniffers,
The Alsatians will go for your throat.

A huddle of men come together,
Volunteers at walking-out time,
To stretch the dogs' legs on their tethers,
Round the perimeter fence in a line.

✻ ✦ ✻ ✦ ✻ ✦ ✻ ✦ ✻ ✦ ✻ ✦ ✻ ✦ ✻ ✦ ✻ ✦ ✻ ✦ ✻ ✦ ✻ ✦

Without fear they lead out the soldiers
To find IEDs[61] by the road
(Disguised within road kill or boulders)
With their sensitive noses as probes.

When a working dog's injured on duty,
The moral desire is to treat.
Would a bullet be kinder to set them free?
Expectations are harder to meet.

For doctors it's not quite so simple,
Though the hero dog's 'one of the crew',
Only vets can treat dogs – what the Dickins[62]
Does the doctor with a sick dog do?

BALLS

THIS VISUAL CONCRETE POEM IS A REFLECTIVE CHALLENGE TO extraordinary advances in military medicine during the Iraq and Afghanistan campaigns, which led to a proven cohort of 'unexpected survivors'. I evaluated these collective advances, many of which I had led, as a PhD thesis and proved them to represent a genuine *Revolution in Military Medical Affairs*.[63] But what is the human cost, the unintended consequence, of surviving devastating injuries that were previously unsurvivable?

Has
medicine
advanced
too
far
that we can save
a man's life who
<u>has</u> only one <u>limb</u>
and no
balls?

●●

If
asked
would <u>most</u>
soldiers
prefer
to
D
I
E
———————————
than to live this life?
THAT TAKES BALLS.

ANIMAL RIGHTS

The United Kingdom has strict laws controlling animal experimentation for human benefit. This includes stringent Home Office licensing of animal experimentation to evaluate benefits from advances in treatment of severe combat injury. The government of the day has a duty of care to protect Service personnel injured in the line of duty, but there is nevertheless an enduring ethical tension with what animal-based research is proportionate and acceptable within continually evolving social norms.

Is it right to use animal models
(A wounded anaesthetised swine)
To show topical blood-clotting agents[64]
Seal a surgical slash in the groin?

Is it right that men go into combat
With no practice to deal with real blood?
Yet you expect the skills for an oil leak
From mechanics who're under your hood.

Is it right to train only in plastic?[65]
Can it simulate reality?
Is the trade-off too morally drastic,
Risking critique of pig cruelty?

Can these rights be compared with each other?
From a pig's life comes the confidence
That a soldier can rescue his brother
From the jaws of predictable death.

ENVIRONMENT
OF WAR

CHEMICAL ALARM

IN FEBRUARY 2003, AROUND 40,000 BRITISH TROOPS ASSEMBLED in tented camps in Kuwait, ahead of the invasion of Iraq and the Second Gulf War. I was the medical director of the first British field hospital deployed into Kuwait, close to the Iraqi border, where we were subjected to Scud missile attack. At this point there was a strong credible threat of chemical weapons.

The reaction to a chemical attack, often at night and signalled by an alarm, was to put on your respirator and chemical protective clothing, then run to the shelter of nearby trenches. The NATO standardised alarm signal for a chemical attack is an intermittent vehicle horn: one second on – one second off.

One second on – one second off,
The vehicle horn was sounding.
Shocked from my sleep I held my breath,
Eyes screwed shut, my heart was pounding.

Under the camp-bed cot I groped,
Shadow friends in green bags flailing.
The rubber straps were where I'd hoped,
"*Gas, gas, gas!*" I screamed, exhaling.

I dragged the charcoal suit on hard,
The roughened lining scratched my skin,
My visibility was marred:
Breath moisture made mask lenses dim.

A stream of silhouetted men
Burst out the tent flap, running low.
Stumbling over feet and guy ropes,
To designated trench they go.

Cursing, sweating, cramped together,
Ears pricked for tell-tale thuds,
For *Patriots*[66] whistling through the ether,
To intercept Iraqi Scuds.[67]

"*De-mask, de-mask!*" A false alarm;
A backing lorry tricked us all.
Return to bed, to pseudo-calm,
Protected by our canvas walls.

FIELD DINING

IN THE CONCENTRATION PHASE PRIOR TO THE IRAQ WAR IN 2003, British troops assembling in Camp Coyote in Kuwait received centralised catering for their evening meal – brown stew (if the colouring was remembered), distributed in insulated boxes. This 'collective catering' was to reduce the chance of foodborne gastroenteritis. The downside was that it was very monotonous. Lunchtime meals consisted of dry rations, which were in short supply: American packet meals were distributed when supplies were low, and when supplies were very low the high calorie arctic ration packs were used.

Oh God it's dinner time again,
What slop will they serve up today?
For thirty days I've had brown stew
(Except once when it was grey).

Poor food here is of course denied
By a lame spokesman in Qatar,
Who's got the nerve to tell the news
Our field catering is five star.

Lunch is the US ready meal
Of vegetable burrito.
It's slimy, plastic, has no taste;
Appetising as a shoe sole.

Salad we want – a lighter diet
(It's bloody hot, the sun's intense).
Instead we're given arctic packs,
A lunatic choice that makes no sense.

Into Iraq on dry rations,
It's *Menu A*, boil in the bag.
'Biscuits, brown'[68] and 'turds in treacle',[69]
Within a week I start to flag.

At last the fresh food does arrive;
Eggs, fruit, veg, fish, meat, poultry, cheese.
But with it an unwanted flood
Of Norwalk virus D and V.[70]

SOLIFUGIT

THE CAMEL SPIDER IS NATIVE TO IRAQ. IT IS NOT ACTUALLY A spider but a member of the genus *Solifugae*, which look like spiders but have ten legs rather than eight. They hide from the sun and run into your shadow (their name means *to flee from the sun*). If you move, they will follow your shadow, giving the impression they are chasing you!

Brown and hairy,
Very scary,
If a spider phobia you've got.
Anaesthetic,
She injects it
To numb your skin (I kid you not).

In your shadow
She will follow,
To keep herself out of the sun.
You may well fear
As she draws near,
You're being chased and you must run.

Solifugit,
Camel spider,
Arachnid urban myths abound.
"As big as plates!"
"It ate my face!"
"It jumped six feet – right off the ground!"

In a mess tin,
With a scorpion,
(Heat the tin over a flame).
Soldiers will bet
On *Solifugit*
To triumph in this lethal game.

This poem has been arranged for a children's choir in original music by Cate Carter.

DEATH OF A CLOCK

WHEN SLEEPING AS HOSPITAL CONSULTANTS IN 8-MAN TENTS,
with only 2 feet between the camp cots (an environment described
in the separate poem *Where am I?*), it felt 'cosy' to say the least. As
someone was invariably disturbed for a clinical reason every night, any
other sleep disruptions were very unwelcome. Even the 'tick-tock' of
an alarm clock became intolerable.

Tick-tock
Sprawled on our camp cots
Tick-tock
Beneath our fly nets
Tick-tock
The tent is airless
Tick-tock
I wouldn't care less
If you'd shut up that ticking clock!

Tick-tock
Each night I'm woken
Tick-tock
To tend bodies broken
Tick-tock
I can't do my best
Tick-tock
If I've had no rest
So shut up that bloody clock!!

Tick-tock
I've lost perspective
Tick-tock
To live and let live
Tick-tock
There's one solution
Bang! Bang!
It's execution
Of that feckin' ticking clock!!!

This poem has been arranged for a children's choir in original music by
Cate Carter. In the arrangement 'bloody clock' and 'feckin clock' are
substituted with 'stupid clock'.

WHERE AM I?

THIS IS A REFLECTION ON THE LIVING AND WORKING CONDITIONS as senior doctor at the relentlessly busy multinational field hospital in Camp Bastion, Helmand Province, Afghanistan, during the summer of 2009.

I live in a high-fenced square surrounded by armed guards;
I eat when I am told, in a communal cookhouse.

I work sixteen hours a day without any respite
Except Sundays, when my day starts one hour later.

I sleep in a seven by three-foot space,
Cramped together with seven other men.

I speak to my family twice a week – for fifteen minutes –
Unless the telephone line is suspended; my calls are monitored.

I have access to some internet sites; my emails are scrutinised;
The use of mobile telephones is banned; alcohol is banned.

Free speech to the media is not allowed;
All contact with the media must be screened.

Transgression of the rules is punishable by fine
Or by transfer to another facility.

Where am I? Not in prison.
Welcome to Camp Bastion, Afghanistan.

HAPPY JOURNEY

THIS POEM FRAMES UNSTATED UNCOMFORTABLE QUESTIONS from the first few days of the Second Gulf War. Why did field hospital staff go to war in a bus (its side ironically stencilled with *Happy Journey*) when other soldiers advanced into Iraq in armoured vehicles? How did the author become abandoned in a border checkpoint on the first night of the war [71], to be collected after the cover of darkness had lifted in a soft-skinned ambulance that became lost in Southern Iraq? Why were there no trenches for the hospital's medical staff, who were in exposed tents beside the bare airfield runway? And why did our own howitzers fire over the hospital from behind a sandbank?

> *Warrior* armoured fighting vehicles,
> *Scimitars* and *4-3-2s*,[72]
> Transported soldiers wrapped in Kevlar,[73]
> Covered from the enemy's view.
>
> Some way down the armoured column
> The *Happy Journey* bus was found,
> Filled with exposed wide-eyed medics
> Without a shield from enemy rounds.
>
> In night convoy (two soft-skinned B.F.As),[74]
> I was to move out from Kuwait.[75]
> Dumped six hours at border checkpoint,
> Then on in daylight, lost and late.

Challenger tanks[76] engage the enemy
Just outside the perimeter berm.[77]
Infantry dive into their trenches,
We drop our lunch, kiss terra firm.

Tracked guns fired a night-time volley,
So loud that I bounced off my cot!
My little tent was caked in cordite,[78]
Protection from Red Cross forgot.

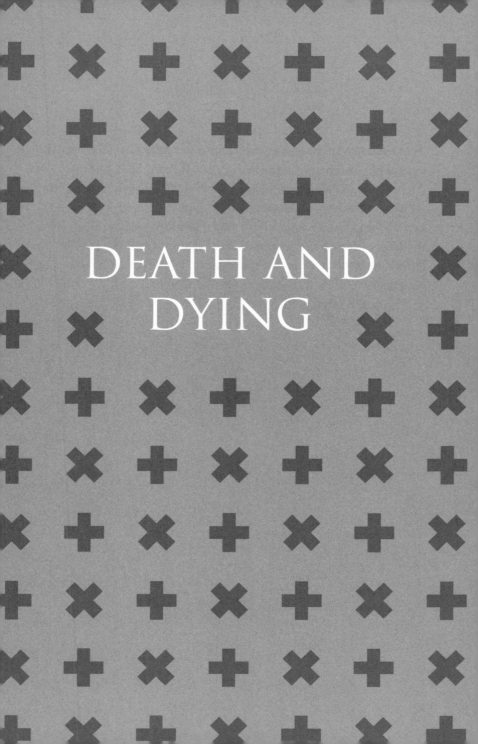

DEATH AND DYING

ROSE COTTAGE

'ROSE COTTAGE' WAS THE EUPHEMISTIC TERM FOR THE TENTED temporary mortuary supporting the British field hospital in Afghanistan. As Consultant Emergency Medicine with responsibility for the mortuary, I directed that no junior medical staff were to examine the dead to issue International Death Certificates. Such was the devastation of the injuries, I felt there was nothing positive for juniors to learn from repeat exposure to a profoundly traumatising experience.

It's 3 a.m. and I'm waiting
Inside a dim lit tent
The nurses call 'Rose Cottage':
It's where the dead are sent.

There's nothing to distract me,
I'm alone with just my thoughts,
And the shadow of a black bag
That I know to hold a corpse.

I'd not say I'm religious,
My logic questions Him,
Yet my overwhelming desire
Is to sing a schoolboy hymn.[79]

I hum the tune inside my head,
Melita[80] comes to mind,
It is a prayer for lost, feared dead,
(There's no hope *his* wife will find).

Why use this euphemism?
To talk freely in veiled speech,
Dissuade juniors from tourism,
And keep horror out of reach.

A HYMN FOR HELMAND

(To the tune of *Melita*, by John B Dykes)

THE CIRCUMSTANCES BEHIND WRITING THIS HYMN ARE described in the poem *Rose Cottage*. Standing in a dimly lit tent in the early hours, suffocated by silence, and with no company other than a partially-filled body bag, I waited for the Chaplain and Royal Military Police so I could conduct the examination of a soldier's paltry remains. I countered the silence by humming *Melita*, a hymn tune remembered from school. You may know it as *Eternal Father Strong to Save* or *For Those in Peril on the Sea*.

For all those soldiers in Helmand[81]
Who sacrificed themselves, we stand
To honour each one's memory
And pray that each one's soul is freed.
   For those who gave their lives we owe
   Love and respect to ever show.

For all those soldiers in Helmand
Whose blood was shed and stained the sand;
Who lost their limbs or lost their mind,
We'll help them heal and peace to find.
   This sacrifice by gallant few,
   Forever we'll remember you.

For all those soldiers in Helmand
Who lived through war to understand
The horror and brutality
Of taking life for liberty:
   Let every soldier hear you say,
   'We value what you do today'.

THE EXTRA LEG

IN SUMMER 2009, IN AFGHANISTAN, MULTIPLE UNIDENTIFIED
bodies and body parts were brought on a flatbed truck to the field
hospital mortuary for victim identification. On this occasion the
multinational staff comprised 50% Danish, 25% British and 25%
American personnel. I was the medical director and senior doctor.

Death brings no feelings anymore,
My humanity has gone.
With every soldier ripped apart,
My soul has become numb.

I'm looking at a bag of parts,
A booted leg is out of place;
We've matched most limbs to chests and guts
And heads without a face.

I'm still left with an extra leg:
A British boot, there's no mistake.
But held beside a legless corpse
It does not match the femur[82] break.

On closer look, the tone of skin
Is darker on the unclaimed limb.
An Afghan soldier soon arrives:
Clothed by Brits – it matches him.

A headless mutilated man
Lies bound by rope, in Danish shirt,
Wounded then tortured by Taliban
And dragged by motorbike through dirt.

I'm working with a Danish team –
Their anxiety is clear.
No M.I.A reports[83] soon seem
To alleviate their fears.

What is the broader message here?
The conflict context metaphor:
Clumsy messy reconstruction
Of a society post-war.

DRESSING THE DEAD

I DEPLOYED IN 2008 TO THE TENTED FIELD HOSPITAL SERVING
the area around Al-Basrah, Southern Iraq. We were on a disused
airfield and part of the expansive Shaibah Log Base. As Consultant
Emergency Medicine and medical director I took responsibility for
attending any dead brought to the temporary mortuary. This poem
records events following one of the frequent mortar or rocket attacks
on the base.

Two bodies lie before me;
Who they are I cannot tell.
Flesh charred by an explosion
Gives a sweet and sickly smell.

A mortar round has landed
On the internet welfare shack
And roasted both *in situ*,
As they emailed family back.

Their faces have been melted,
No dog tags round their necks,
Only bits of clothing remnants
To help ID by the med techs.[84]

Their limbs have all contracted,
Twisted postures fixed in death.
As we force their legs out straight,
Exhaled bubbles mimic breath.

My arms are caked in charcoal
From where they've rubbed on skin.
My desert boots are soiled with blood
And destined for the bin.

The indignity's completed:
Bodies bound and sealed in bags.
The cold *Grim Reefer*[85] names the souls
With 'male', 'large', 'unknown' tags.

Two medics are affected
By what they've seen and done.
I counsel them though also numbed
By wounds from bomb and gun.

A PREMONITION OF DEATH

THIS POEM IS INSPIRED BY A CRITICALLY INJURED SOLDIER whom I triaged as he was lifted from the ambulance at the field hospital entrance. He was pale, bloody, and tears lay on his cheeks. He was close to death: 'circling the drain'. I leant over the stretcher to reassure him and heard him tell me, *"I'm never going to see my wife and son again"*. With my own wife and son at home, this brought a lump to my throat. Notably, the first thing he asked was, *"You are not the priest are you?"*, which rather confirmed that he knew he was dying and reminded me to effectively identify myself to a patient!

I directed the soldier to be moved straight onto the operating table where he immediately received a massive blood transfusion and life-saving surgery. Later that day, when I visited intensive care, the patient was propped up in bed, minus his legs, but talking to his wife by satellite phone. This was a genuinely extraordinary recovery.

"Am I going to die?" the soldier said,
Eyes widened with fear, sweat on his forehead.
He gripped tight the stretcher, wet with his blood,
Lifted his head as much as he could,
Saw where his legs once were, hanging in shreds.

"No, you're not going to die," the Army nurse said,
Words calm and soothing, close to his ear,
As if only he should be able to hear,
He turned and with trusting face looked straight at her,
Vulnerable and childlike he appeared on the bed.

"Not on my shift!" the team leader said,
His authority clear from the foot of the bed.
*"Try not to worry – you're in safe hands now,
You'll wake up at home, with family round you."*
Gasman[86] nodded, took control of the head.

"Is he going to die?" his best friend said,
His face, from the same blast, abraded and red,
"We'll do our best – he's as bad as it gets."
Less positive tone is used so it sets
Conditions to tell him his best friend is dead.

Do I know he will die with wounds like this?
I can't reliably predict with ISS:[87]
I do know the 'triad' must not develop,[88]
Or in death's arms he *will* be enveloped.
No rescue from that clinical abyss.

POLITICS

AMPUTEE

WRITTEN IN 2006, THIS POEM REFERS TO THE THEN CURRENT criticism about inadequate compensation for limb loss in combat injury. It was written after I visited the Brook Army Medical Center in San Antonio and was inspired by the positive attitude of a recovering veteran, who had limb loss and facial scarring from burns. This veteran had returned to the wards to support those struggling to adapt to their circumstances in the early phases of recovery. Compensation for British soldiers within the *Armed Forces Compensation Scheme* is now carefully matched to injury severity and functional disability.

Is he less of a man
Missing legs, amputated?
Compensation a sham:
Only one limb's been rated.

By the pains from his stumps
Every night he is woken.
He cries out, his hand held,
Nursing words softly spoken.

New prosthetics displace
Old aesthetics, and should
Give more function than Ace
Pilots' legs of hard wood.[89]

They don't want your pity,
Your uncomfortable smiles.
War's children aren't pretty
But they're proud and alive.

Can he go back to work
With one eye or one hand?
Fly a desk as a clerk,
Or will this be too bland?

Will he hanker for action
Red tape will deny?
Will hope turn to rancour,
Will he no longer try?

Will a Purple Heart[90] open
A jar or a tin,
Or a door to a job
A more able man's in?

Will his girlfriend stick by him
Or marry from guilt?
Can she live with burns scarring
A face to rebuild?

In two years he returns
To wards where he lay,
New wife on his good arm
Big smile on his face.

To raw comrades fearful
Their lives are destroyed,
This champion of hope
Is bitterness devoid.

YOU'RE GOING TO WAR SO WORRY

In 2003, a Western coalition of the willing, led by the United States, went to war with Saddam Hussein's Ba'athist regime in Iraq. The political rationale presented by US to the United Nations was 'credible intelligence' of a programme to develop weapons of mass destruction, in contravention to UN Resolution 1441, together with Iraq's involvement in activities to support terrorist training. The Chilcot Inquiry began in 2009 to codify the lessons learned from this Iraq campaign for UK government and Defence. This poem was written while I was deployed as the medical director and Emergency Medicine Consultant for the field hospital in Kuwait, during the pre-war concentration phase, when I was experiencing serial challenges in equipment availability, decision-making and logistics.

"You cannot have a pistol",
On advance into Iraq:
"Not enough to go around, sir",
Nor a plate to shield my back.
You're going to war so worry
That you're missing vital kit.
From Blair there'll be no "Sorry!"
For your body bag of bits.

My gas mask training filter
Cannot cope with nerve agent.
"A real one's out in theatre" –[91]
For this lie, who's negligent?
You're going to war so worry

You'll not be fully prepared.
At home Blair's watching telly
But, unlike you, isn't scared.

The threat of smallpox virus
Is a real and present fear.
Why promised vaccination
Isn't given isn't clear.
You're going to war so worry,
Even if you conquer fear,
Nightmares, flash backs, P.T.S.D,[92]
May wreck your life forever.

Twenty-thousand Combo-Pens
(A chemical antidote),[93]
I must reassure the men
Will work though out of date.
You're going to war so worry
There's no job when you come home.[94]
Your employer has no conscience
Nor respect for what you've done.

Our re-supply is no good;
It is slower than the post.
Mum's cake reached here before the blood,[95]
But thankfully at no cost.
You're going to war so worry,
Whines and moans will be ignored.
You risk your life for country
But the country has grown bored.

WITHDRAWAL FROM BASRA

OPERATION TELIC IS THE NAME ASSIGNED TO THE CAMPAIGN in Iraq that began on 19 March 2003 with the invasion in Iraq, and completed on 3 September 2011. Most troops were drawn down in 2009. I served during concentration and warfighting phases (rotating sequentially through 22, 33 and 34 Field Hospitals in Kuwait then into Iraq, in what I refer to as 'The Field Hospital Grand Tour'), then as field hospital Consultant Emergency Medicine and Hospital Clinical Director in 2004, 2006 and 2008. In a statistic that no-one would envy, I was at the field hospital in Al-Basrah to certify the deaths of both the first British soldier in 2003 and the hundredth, in 2006.

When the papers are compelling
And the stark truth they are telling
Is that British Forces have now lost control.
There is only one real option
For the guiding coalition:
Accept defeat and, fighting, make withdrawal.

When the only reason to stay
Is the date to leave to delay
It is difficult to justify more deaths.
Chinese rockets rain down each day
On Basra airport where we all pray
That our tour will end and we'll survive this mess.

Breeze block blast walls round our beds,[96]
The mortar siren fills our heads,
Another fearful sleepless night comes to an end.
But how to cope with all this stress?
Will comrades gossip and think less
Of those broken soldiers who go round the bend?

RAMP CEREMONY

In the early phases of the Iraq and Afghanistan campaigns, media attention for those killed on active service centred on the ceremony of the body being moved from aircraft to the waiting hearse – the 'Ramp Ceremony'. It was regularly attended by political figures. As these campaigns continued, the media also focused on the public display of grief and appreciation in the village of Wootton Bassett[97] (granted the prefix *Royal* in October 2011), which was on the route from RAF Brize Norton to Oxford, where post-mortem examination was carried out.

Through grey cloud the plane descended
(Though summer's day, the sky was dark),
The tailgate dropped as props' roar ended,
Then the Light Blue[98] band struck deathly march.

A slow procession, coffins borne
By hatless friends, their faces set,
A scene now played out far too often,
With silence by the crowd was met.

Prominent elected faces
Stood conspicuously at the front;
With feign concern for young life wasted,
Bare-chested[99] they parade their guilt.

TV cameras caught the moment:
Frames of grief beamed round the world.
No care for hearing Blair's lament,[100]
Hypocrisy in death unfurled.

The next day and another plane,
From Cyprus (a car accident),
No band, no guests, a corporate shame,
No respect to the occasion lent.

For this is how we treat our dead
When serving, but when not at war:
No pomp, no flag, plain box of lead,
A blip in monthly stats, no more.

PARADOX OF THE INJURED

IF YOU HAVE WATCHED PROFESSIONAL SOCCER YOU WILL BE familiar with how players exaggerate an injury, falling dramatically to the ground apparently in severe pain before getting up to continue the game, seemingly unaffected. For those truly injured and carried off the pitch, there is a good deal less drama but clear distress, perhaps from immediate concern about how the injury might affect their playing career.

Conversely, for soldiers seriously injured in combat, a paradoxical relief has been observed when the implications of being injured lead to an escape from the misery and anxiety of war.

A footballer nudged in the back
Falls as cut by a skilled lumberjack,
Then writhes on the ground
(With no injury found)
Bouncing up to return to attack.

From the soldier who steps on a mine,
Not a moan, nor a whimper or whine.
This might be explained
That, despite being maimed,
He'll be heading back home from the line.

The pundits talk 'heroes' and 'battle',
When such banter just serves to belittle
The true sacrifice
Through our soldiers' lives,
In defence of the right to this prattle.

All the footballer leaves on the pitch
Is sportsmanship, pride and his spit.
Not the blood, limbs and guts
Or even his nuts,
When a soldier has been blown to bits.

This is something we already know
From experience in Anzio,
Where Beecher[101] had seen
Not a pipe nor a scream,
After 'Blighty'[102] that would send lads home.

It is true these are apples and pears,
Their miseries cannot compare.
The sportsman will fear
He has lost his career,
While the soldier now has hope to bear.

MILITARY HUMANITARIANISM

This poem explores the tension between military interaction with the host country's civil population and the interaction of agencies on the ground that provide humanitarian aid. It refers to the cornerstone principles of International Humanitarian Law (humanity, neutrality, impartiality, independence) and asks whether the military can ever fulfil these criteria. There are black, white and also grey areas, where the use of language becomes important in maintaining boundaries of perceived responsibility and legitimacy.

Is 'military humanitarianism' an oxymoron?
Is treating the child of a village elder 'humanitarian',
Or is it simply using medicine
As a weapon
To support the military mission objectives?

How can an army be regarded as humanitarian
When by definition it imposes an external set of values?
It is not neutral; it is not impartial.
It is not inclusive of everyone's needs.
Except when it supports a disaster relief operation.

Calling military activities 'humanitarian' creates friction
Between the military and the *bona fide* aid agencies.
Could this not be simply defused
By a better use of language,
By restricting the term to genuinely humanitarian tasks?

The military must accept that it has wrongly adopted this term,
That its use tarnishes the aid agencies and threatens their
    neutrality.
But is the military mind mature enough?
Can the dogma of doctrine be displaced by pragmatism?
Or is the military to be condemned by literary inflexibility?

REMEMBRANCE

THE BLACK SNAKE

THOSE WHO LIVED THROUGH THE IRAQ CONFLICT OF 2003–2009 and the Afghanistan conflict of 2002–2014 will recall television images showing convoys of hearses bearing coffins draped with Union flags, as they drove through the Oxfordshire village of Royal Wootton Bassett in slow procession from RAF Brize Norton to post-mortem examination under jurisdiction of the Oxford Coroner.

Long and black
With high gloss back
Is our most deadly snake.
Through glass belly,
The mourners see
Britain on the caskets draped.

The Legion's[103] flags
With respect sag,
Dipping as the snake glides by.
A petal shower
Forms a thin cover
As families, in silence, cry.

This wooden meal,
Far from unreal's
A consequence of modern war;
Where choice, not need,
Impels we feed
The virtuous cycle to endure.

ANNIVERSARY

For anyone who has experienced a major traumatic event an anniversary is a difficult time. Some are collectively commemorated, so that their significance is felt across a community or nation. I find personal meaning in the anniversary of the Musgrave Park Hospital bombing in Belfast, on 2 November 1991 when, as the resident physician, I assumed the role of medical commander.[104] This was an inflection point in my career, which provided me with enduring motivation to develop national and international standards in pre-hospital emergency care and disaster medicine. In 2021, as Surgeon General, I arranged a thirty-year commemoration. Lest we forget.

Where were you on 9/11?[105]
Our generation knows.
And for Londoners each 7/7[106]
A wound is yet to close.

Each year the victims sense again
What they're trying to forget:
A smell… a taste… the sounds of pain;
For things not done – regret.

Their lives have since been redefined
By their watershed event;
Before or after, in their mind,
They frame all life's content.

But public memory is short
For non-politicised events;
Attention of the press being caught
And held by extremist intent.

Forgotten are those lesser hells
From act of God or accident,
Whose anniversaries don't sell
Despite the parallel torment.

Am I one of those 'lesser' men?
Experience my jail.
It was '91, in Belfast, when
Bang! went my hospital.

What has 'life after' meant for me?
What's been my own catharsis?
To write, and teach the world to be
Prepared for MASCAL[107] crisis.

FLAG OF REMEMBRANCE

I CONSTRUCTED THIS *FLAG OF REMEMBRANCE* ON MICROSOFT PowerPoint® while deployed in Afghanistan during Gordon Brown's premiership (2007–2010). I met the Prime Minister when he visited the field hospital to speak directly to injured British troops. I had previously met Prime Minister Tony Blair when he visited the Royal Centre for Defence Medicine, Birmingham, where I was the military clinical director.

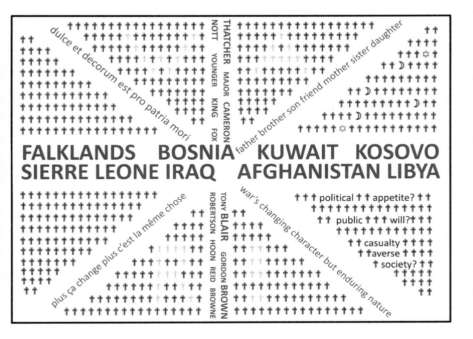

FALKLANDS BOSNIA KUWAIT KOSOVO
SIERRE LEONE IRAQ AFGHANISTAN LIBYA

GHOSTS OF NORMANDY

THIS POEM WAS INSPIRED BY A 'BATTLEFIELD TOUR' OF THE Normandy beaches as part of the Advanced Command and Staff Course in 2011. From the beach I looked up at the defensive positions on the steep surrounding ridge, then later looked down from the hillside concrete bunker, from which the withering enfilade of machinegun fire had cut down the landing troops.

On 'Bloody Omaha'
For sixty years they've roamed,
Enduring echoes of a war,
Their peace yet to be found.

Surviving concrete bunkers
Hold the souls of Germany's sons,
In silence, poised and hunkered
Over ethereal guns.

For they are the opposing ghosts,
The remnants of the lives
Of brave men fighting at their posts
For their freedom and their wives.

The sea is long-since blue again,
All ferrous pigment[108] washed away,
The stench of death, the cries of pain,
A distant fading memory.

Yet standing on the beach today,
Detached by half a century,
I close my eyes and I can see
The lasting ghosts of Normandy.

IN MEMORIAM OF DR ROSS

In 2023, as part of an official visit to Serbia (as UK Surgeon General and elected Chair of the Committee of Chiefs of Military Medical Services in NATO) I laid a wreath at the graves of medical staff from the Scottish field hospital who died tending to Serbian victims of the typhus epidemic during the First World War. Red Cross student volunteers kept the memorial spotless. I was asked to write something as a lasting memory, to be read at the enduring annual ceremony: this was first read at her graveside on 14 February 2024.

I also read this poem, to bring the story to a new generation, at the Scottish National War Memorial on 2 December 2023 in the ceremony to mark the formation of 215 (Scottish) Multirole Medical Regiment from the amalgamation of 205 Field Hospital and 225 (Scottish) Medical Regiment.

> Here rests the soul of Doctor Ross,
> She made the highest sacrifice,
> Her cherished grave gathers no moss,
> A victim of the typhus lice.
>
> Today she's tended by Red Cross:
> Young volunteers, new lives inspired
> By actions to reduce Serb loss,
> Her legacy far from expired.
>
> We remember you,
> Elizabeth Ross.[109]

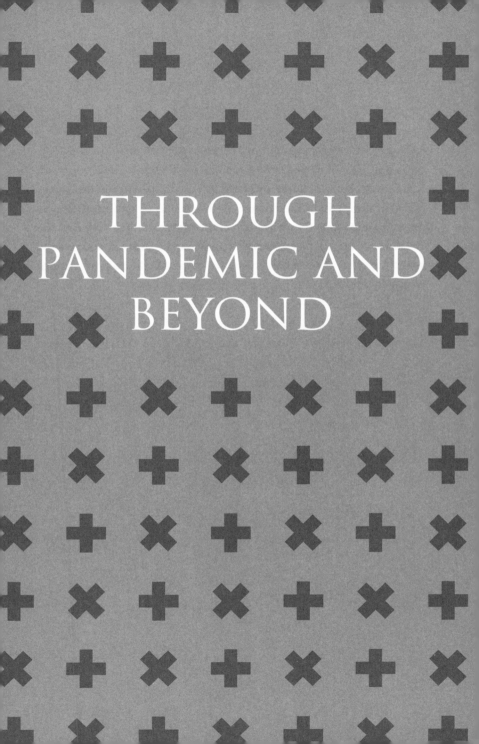

THROUGH PANDEMIC AND BEYOND

COVID FUNERAL

IN 2020, MY PARENTS WERE HOSPITALISED FOR MONTHS DURING the height of the Covid-19 pandemic, moving from ward to ward, from hospital to care home and back to hospital. They died two weeks apart, in separation. Attendance at their bedside had been heavily restricted except at the end of life. Attendance at their funerals was equally restricted. It is a miserable story that was replicated across the country. Except in certain walks of life, where the enforced restrictions were not followed.

The rules allowed just twenty
Their last respects to pay,
The chapel largely empty
At Dad's funeral today.

We'd watched my father wither
In occasional photographs,
Delay, neglect and dither
Had caused setback and relapse.

Each Thursday night we public
Stood outside and clapped for care,
But inside I just felt sick –
To have slapped them would be fair.

Elsewhere we learned the same rules
Some MPs did not obey:
They took us all for Covid fools,
Uncovered by Sue Gray.[110]

"It's time to move on", you know,
No accountability here;
Nor trust, nor shame – bravado
To twist the public's ear.

COVID PPE

DURING THE COVID-19 PANDEMIC THERE WAS A SHORTAGE OF personal protective equipment for hospitals and care homes. Large government contracts were placed, which delivered PPE that in some cases failed to meet quality or safety standards and was unusable.

Can't you see
That we need
PPE?

PPE
Guarantees
My safety.

Must I ask
For a mask
In my task?

I must don
An apron –
But there's none.

If I die
Will they try
To deny

That they bought
Without thought
The wrong sort?

Now we're stuck
With this muck –
What the f*ck

Can we do
Before you,
You and you

Swallow fear
As you wear
This sh*t gear.

BLUE OVER YELLOW

BLUE OVER YELLOW ARE THE STRIPES OF THE UKRAINIAN FLAG.
An inverted flag, in this case yellow over blue, is an internationally
recognised distress signal – or, in certain circumstances, a signal of protest.

Blue over yellow:
Sky over wheat field.
Though field guns bellow,
No ground will they yield.

Blue over yellow:
Sun rises in sky.
We salute fellows
With shared values, who die.

Blue over yellow:
Black Sea meets the beach,
Resistance below
Keeps freedom in reach.

Yellow over blue:
A sign of distress,
While a battling few
Fight those who oppress.

Yellow over blue:
For nation they fight.
Two versions of true:
Just one will yield light.

With these two colours
Our flags must unite,
To combat dishonour
That madness incites.

ALL THINGS SAD AND PITIFUL

THIS POEM PARODIES THE POPULAR HYMN *ALL THINGS BRIGHT and Beautiful*. If a higher being is believed responsible for all the world's good, does that belief extend to them having tolerance, or even responsibility, for all the bad?

At the time of writing in 2023 the Russo–Ukraine war had been raging for 18 months and the Israel–Hamas war had just begun with unprecedented missile bombardment and terrorist attack on Israeli civilians in the south of the country.

[To the tune *All Things Bright and Beautiful* by Cecil Frances Alexander and William Henry Monk]

All things sad and pitiful,
All consequence of war;
All grades of pain and suffering,
The Lord God knows them all.
Each cluster bomb exploded,
Each barrel bomb of gas,
Each child by war who's orphaned,
The ownership He has.

All hate, lies and ignorance,
All envy, vice and greed;
All negative behaviours,
In mankind He did seed.
Each fingernail extracted,
Each beating to confess;
He made all evil bastards,
Whose deeds must He still bless?

All things trite and trivial,
All arrogance supreme;
All bloated over-confidence
And misplaced self-esteem.
Each evil regime leader
And flagrant psychopath
Who builds a nuclear arsenal,
And risks global blood bath.

All things sad and pitiful,
All consequence of war;
All grades of pain and suffering,
The Lord God knows them all.
We owe it to our children
To stop all future war
And prevent conflagration
Consuming one and all.

All those wise and wonderful,
All people fabulous,
Award Him credit plentiful
For making them and us.
As-well.[111]

FALSE ASSUMPTIONS OF SUICIDE

EVERY SUICIDE OF A SERVING SOLDIER, SAILOR OR AVIATOR IS acutely felt and perhaps receives greater media attention than an equally tragic event in the civilian community. The causes of suicide of serving and veteran personnel are complex, and commonly held misconceptions exist – in particular, that suicide is confined to young men, that it is invariably related to experience on deployment, and that it is invariably underpinned by mental ill-health. The evidence reveals that these are by no means pre-requisite causes.

You can make the false assumption
It's experience on tour
That drives soldiers to distraction,
To then cope with life no more.

You can make the false assumption
They will display herald signs[112]
(Odd behaviour or depression),
Although often they'll seem fine.

You can make the false assumption
There is time enough to act,
When they're driven by compulsion
With a rational logic lack.

You can make the false assumption
That they're mentally unwell,
When relationships, addiction,[113]
Are more likely alarm bells.

You can make the false assumption
Everyone wants to be saved,
Yet concealment or deception
Hides intent until too late.

You can make the false assumption
It is confined to young men,
When new data shows inclusion
Of age, cap-badge,[114] and women.

Therefore make the *right* assertions
On what causes suicide,
So we focus our attention
On prevention Service-wide.

WE ARE HERE

WE ARE HERE IS WRITTEN AS A CONVERSATION IN LYRICAL
form, to be sung between a serviceman and his wife. The choice of
a male expressing shame, fear, loneliness and despair is deliberate,
and intended to represent the 'bottling up' of male emotion, lived
experience of stigma, and concern about the potential impact on a
career of admitting mental ill-health, which has been observed in the
armed forces. Such feelings are, of course, not gender-specific and the
voices in this conversation can be transposed.[115]

The armed forces have invested considerable formal effort to build
personal resilience from the point of joining, to remove stigma, and
to provide a safe environment for both listening and asking for help.

Male Solo or Choir   *Female Choir*

I am ashamed,
I am afraid
I will lose everything
That we've both made.

                    Military wives,
                    Rock of your lives,
                    We'll always be there for you,
                    Take care and help see you through.

I feel alone,
I'm in despair,
I can't see my way out…
Life's so unfair.

Military wives,
Rock of your lives,
We'll always be there for you,
Take care and help see you through.

Army has had
All my best years,
When I cry every night
They won't hear.

Military wives,
Rock of your lives,
We'll always be there for you,
Take care and help see you through.

When I've had thoughts
To take my life,
I just think of my kids
And my wife.

There is no shame,
It is okay,
What you've suffered
Has made you this way.

Don't bottle it up,
Do shed your tears,
You can trust us to share
Doubts and fears.

Military wives,
Rock of our lives,
We're ever thankful to you
For always helping us through:
Our military wives.

Military wives,
Rock of your lives,
We'll always be there for you,
Take care and help see you through:
Your military wives!

ABOUT THE AUTHOR

Major General Tim Hodgetts CB CBE KHS OStJ DL
DSc PhD MMEd MBA CMgr FRCP FRCSEd FRCEM FFPH
FIMCRCSEd FEPS FCMI FRGS

TIM HODGETTS WAS COMMISSIONED IN THE ARMY IN 1983, and qualified with distinction from Westminster Medical School, London, in 1986. Early postings were to military hospitals in Hannover, Woolwich, Northern Ireland and Aldershot, after which he underwent specialist training in Emergency Medicine (EM) in Manchester and Sydney. He became an EM consultant in 1995 and has been an honorary university professor since 1998. Tim served as Head of the Army Medical Services and Commissioner at the Royal Hospital Chelsea from 2018 to 2021, during the Covid-19 pandemic. In 2021, he was appointed Surgeon General of the United Kingdom for three years and, in parallel, elected by the nations to be Chair of the Committee of Chiefs of Military Medical Services in NATO. He was separately appointed as Master General of the Army Medical Services from 2022, and as Deputy Lieutenant for the County of West Midlands from 2023. He is co-founder of the charity *citizenAID*, and a trustee of London's Air Ambulance and The Poppy Factory.

Tim has deployed extensively: in Northern Ireland, Kosovo, Oman, four tours of Iraq and three of Afghanistan. On six overseas tours he was Medical Director of the field hospital. In 1999, he was made Officer of the Order of St John after leading the first operational deployment of the EM speciality to Kosovo, and, in tandem, building an emergency department for the country's principal hospital in Pristina. In 2009, Tim was made Commander of the British Empire for his decade of work to revolutionise combat casualty outcomes through new concepts, equipment, training, guidelines and governance; and, in 2023, he was made Companion of the Order of the Bath for his work to support the Covid pandemic and for leadership of the international military medical effort within NATO to support Ukraine. In 2010, he received the Danish Defence Medal for Meritorious Service for his role as Medical Director of the Danish field hospital in Afghanistan during an extended high-intensity period of casualties; and, in 2022, he was inducted into the Order of Military Medical Merit of the United States Army. Tim was Queen's Honorary Physician from 2004 to 2010 and has been Queen's Honorary Surgeon then King's Honorary Surgeon since 2018.

Tim has been described in a British Medical Association dossier as one of the most innovative doctors in the country. In 2006, he was recognised as Hospital Doctor of the Year across the NHS. He lives in Birmingham with his wife, Mags, and has a grown-up son, Jack.

ENDNOTES

....

1 Hodgetts TJ, Nee PA., *Rhythms in Rhyme* in the Journal of the British Association for Immediate Care 1993; 16:42.

2 'Tube': the endotracheal breathing tube inserted to enable artificial ventilation.

3 'IV': intravenous line, by which to administer the 1mg in 10mls of adrenaline, often via pre-filled syringe.

4 '200, 200, 360': The first three sequential shocks from a defibrillator, measured in joules.

5 www.citizenaid.org

6 World in Union is the anthem of the Rugby Union World Cup Final: 30 years on it still triggers memories of 2 November 1991.

7 Twickenham Stadium: the recognised home of England Rugby.

8 These exams included the Diploma in Immediate Medical Care of the Royal College of Surgeons of Edinburgh, in its first year of establishment. I had turned the preparation for this exam into my first book, published in 1990, which included an exercise for how to manage multiple casualties from a bomb. I had sketched the line drawings of the casualties myself. A case of life imitating art.

9 Accident and Emergency.

10 Intensive Therapy Unit.

11 A separate landline telephone system that connected military establishments, including official housing. I had a military house with a military phone in London. The civilian telephone system (British Telecom) could not be used in the immediate aftermath of the bomb, only the military system.

12 I left as planned the following morning at 7 a.m. The bomb was on my last day of duty, and even such an event did not alter the pre-determined roulement of staff.

13 Those who lost their lives were WO2 Philip Cross, Royal Army Medical Corps,

and Driver Craig Pantry, Royal Corps of Transport. Lest we forget.

14 The Platinum Ten Minutes of opportunity to treat life-threatening injuries.

15 A structured message of nine separate components used when requesting a helicopter to retrieve a casualty.

16 Shrimp shells contain the active agent chitosan that promotes blood clotting. Soldiers are issued with chitosan dressings.

17 6 ribs down identifies the site between the 5th and 6th ribs, where a chest drain is inserted to treat a collapsed lung.

18 Saline: a salt solution used to temporarily replace lost blood during resuscitation.

19 Intra-Osseous: a metal needle is drilled into the bone to administer drugs and fluids into the marrow cavity. It effects rapid, safe resuscitation in the pre-hospital military environment, particularly if the veins collapse due to low circulating blood volume, making it difficult to insert an intravenous cannula.

20 Four bags of universal donor blood and four of plasma, brought to the Emergency Department (ED) in anticipation of patients with life-threatening bleeding.

21 A journalist located with a unit and authorised to report for a period of days to months.

22 Personal Protective Equipment: in ED this means a minimum of surgical gloves, lead gown and plastic apron.

23 "Wheels up" communicates that the helicopter has taken off.

24 Diastole: the heart's resting phase when it fills with blood before contracting.

25 Baron Dominique Larrey was Napoleon's Surgeon Marshall. He introduced the *ambulance volante* (flying ambulance) to carry the wounded from the battlefield to

field hospital. 'Larrey's new cart' refers to the modern battlefield helicopter.

26 Oedema refers to airway swelling, often resulting from burn when hot gases are inhaled.

27 *The T*4 category identifies casualties who will not survive even if treated – also known as the 'expectant' category.

28 Ghandi ideal: the major incident mantra to "do the best for the most". Gandhi disagreed, as the 'most' may theoretically only be 51%. His preferred mantra was to "do the best for all".

29 7.62 is the calibre, in millimetres, of the machine gun bullets.

30 MANPAD is a shoulder launched missile system.

31 Taliban (also Taleban): a political and religious faction established in Afghanistan from the mid-1990s.

32 Rocket Propelled Grenade – a favoured weapon of terrorists/insurgents in Iraq and Afghanistan conflicts. When fired out to its maximum range (900m) the safety fuse results in detonation: this has been capitalised upon to produce an indirect proximity weapon for attacking aircraft.

33 Surface to Air Missile.

34 Apache is a 2-crew attack helicopter.

35 Hellfire is the missile system on Apache.

36 Kevlar is the armour plating of the helicopter.

37 Mini-gun is a machine gun mounted on the CH47 (Chinook) helicopter side-door, that fires 1000 rounds per minute.

38 Internal radio communications (or lack of them for medical crew).

39 Camp Bastion, the British base in Helmand Province that hosted an increasingly sophisticated field hospital 2006–2014.

40 A and E, Accident and Emergency: now more commonly ED, the Emergency Department.

41 Gasman is common slang for an anaesthetist or anaesthesiologist of any gender.

42 MEDPLAN: military abbreviation for Medical Plan.

43 Kabul, the capital of Afghanistan, was the main airhead in 2002: Bagram Airbase was just north of Kabul.

44 Loss of Consciousness.

45 Lieutenant John Chard VC: Royal Engineers' officer commanding the British outpost at Rorke's Drift, in 1879, when it was overwhelmed by the Zulu army.

46 Oman was where 24000 British troops had been practicing desert manoeuvres on *Exercise Saif Sareea II*, summer 2001.

47 'Man' is a deliberate juxtaposition to 'Oman', while noting that even in 2002 language was much less gender inclusive.

48 Radiology Technician/Radiographer.

49 Vent: a ventilator to support breathing. An X-ray is required after emergency ventilation to determine lung pathology and check the position of the tube in the trachea.

50 Telemedicine is the data transfer (X-rays, CT scans, vital signs, video conferencing) from a remote site to a central hub of expertise for advice. However, its simplest form remains using the telephone to seek verbal advice.

51 The military abbreviation for Directing Staff Solution – the 'ideal' or 'model' solution.

52 "The solution to pollution is dilution" is a Trauma Rule (Hodgetts T., Turner L., *Trauma Rules 2*. London: Blackwell, 2006).

53 Critical Care Air Support Team – the intensive care capability to fly ventilated patients from an overseas field hospital back home to an NHS hospital.

54 Bio-warfare: a strong possibility of a biological warfare attack was considered early in the outbreak.

55 Cefotaxime: a broad-spectrum antibiotic for serious infections when the cause is not yet known.

56 Plasma was needed when a ventilated patient developed abnormal blood clotting while waiting for evacuation (Disseminated Intravascular Coagulopathy, or DIC).

57 A virus is too small to see on a standard light microscope (magnifies up to 2000 times) but requires an electron microscope, which magnifies up to 10 million times.

58 Norovirus is spread through aerosolised vomit and faeces, which has been responsible for outbreaks of diarrhoea and vomiting in crowded institutions such as civilian hospitals, cruise ships and schools. We were surprised to identify a new viral strain of norovirus that had never been reported, and which produced the severe complications of meningitis and coma in this outbreak. This was reported as an "Outbreak of acute gastroenteritis associated with Norwalk-like viruses among British military personnel—Afghanistan, May 2002" in *MMWR Morbidity and Mortality Weekly Report*, 2002; 51: 477–9.

59 The Hippocratic Oath, traditionally sworn by doctors on qualification.

60 Troops in Contact (*pronounced* 'tick').

61 Improvised Explosive Devices.

62 'Dickins' refers to Maria Dickin CBE, founder of the People's Dispensary for Sick Animals (PDSA), who introduced the Dickin Medal in 1943 in recognition for animal gallantry. The medal has come to be regarded as the animal's Victoria Cross.

63 This poem was exhibited at the National Army Museum *Unseen Enemy* exhibition in 2013. The evidence of the contemporary 'Revolution in Military Medical Affairs' – the modern transformation of combat casualty care outcomes as they occurred in the United Kingdom – was published in 2012 as a PhD thesis by the author, Tim Hodgetts, entitled *A revolutionary approach to improving combat casualty care*. The thesis is available in open access on-line at https://openaccess.city.ac.uk/id/eprint/2040/

64 Topical blood clotting agent: a new generation of 'topical haemostatic' treatments emerged c.2003: powders or bandages were impregnated with an active ingredient to promote blood clotting. An 'industry standard' was needed to allow meaningful comparison in international research studies, which became a controlled

groin incision (slash in the groin) in an anaesthetised pig, which cut through the blood vessels, and was located too high on the limb to be controlled with a tourniquet. The initial stimulus for developing this animal model was the death of an American soldier in Mogadishu from a groin wound, survivable had the ability to control the bleeding been available. It is documented in *Black Hawk Down*, by Mark Bowden

65 UK law prohibits using live animals for training purposes although, at time of writing, it is permitted in some allied countries. In the UK creative alternatives have been devised to allow combat medics the experience of controlling 'real' bleeding in inert models utilising butchered meat. I introduced this model in the Iraq field hospital, in 2004, using pork belly from the field kitchen and date-expired human blood that would have been incinerated.

See *A realistic model for catastrophic bleeding training*, Moorhouse I *et al.*, available at https://pubmed.ncbi.nlm.nih.gov/17896537/

66 US radar-guided surface to air anti-missile system.

67 Vehicle-launched ballistic missiles with a range of several hundred kilometres.

68 The very dry oatmeal biscuit in ration packs.

69 Sealed plastic bag of pudding pieces in a toffee sauce, cooked by boiling the bag.

70 *Norwalk virus D and V* refers to the outbreaks of diarrhoea and vomiting seen when large numbers of people are accommodated close together (universities, hospitals, cruise ships, military barracks

71 Link this experience to the first verse of *You're Going to War So Worry*.

72 *Warrior, Scimitar* and *432* (pronounced four three two) are all armoured vehicles used by the British Army during the Gulf War 2003. *Warrior* and *432* were used as armoured personnel carriers (APCs); *Scimitar* was a reconnaissance vehicle.

73 A bullet-resistant material.

74 BFA is the Landrover Battlefield Ambulance, which is soft skinned – that is, no protective armour.

75 Kuwait was the country in which British troops concentrated before the invasion of Iraq in March 2003. I was assigned to 22 Field Hospital in Kuwait at the start of the concentration pre-war phase: this was in Camp COYOTE. I moved forward independently to join up with 34 Field Hospital, who had assembled separately in Camp FOX.

76 Challenger is the British Army's main battle tank.

77 Berm is a sandbank, artificially created by bulldozer to provide protection for tented facilities in desert locations.

78 Cordite is a propellant in military firearms, although for strict accuracy it has been replaced by more modern propellants. "Modern ammunition propellant" does not quite scan within the verse, so this is poetic licence.

79 I attended Woodhouse Grove School, near Bradford in West Yorkshire, which was established in 1812 as a school for the sons of Methodist ministers. It retained a strong religious component in the curriculum, with daily assemblies and weekly services in the school's chapel that included singing hymns.

80 'Melita' is the tune to the hymn 'Eternal Father, Strong to Save' (also known as 'For Those in Peril on the Sea'). Inspired by this experience while waiting in Rose Cottage, I wrote *A Hymn for Helmand* to this tune in the following days.

81 Helmand Province in Southern Afghanistan was the centre of gravity for British military troops deployed in the 2002–2014 NATO-led coalition.

82 Thigh bone.

83 MIA means Missing in Action.

84 Combat Medical Technician, a soldier professionally trained as a medic.

85 The name given to the refrigerated ISO container (or "reefer") that is used as a temporary mortuary.

86 Common slang for an anaesthetist or anaesthesiologist (any gender).

87 ISS (pronounced as a single word) is the Injury Severity Score, an internationally accepted tool to predict outcome from serious injury: but it regularly overestimates the survival from combat-related injury. We found the New Injury Severity Score (NISS) to be a more reliable predictor for our military patients. Nevertheless, both tools are retrospective and currently only clinical intuition from deep experience will tell you the likelihood of survival.

88 The 'lethal triad' is the combination of coagulopathy (inability of the blood to clot), hypothermia (low body temperature) and acidosis (excessive acidity of the blood) that is a complication of serious injury and, if not avoided or treated promptly and aggressively, will often mark a spiralling deterioration to death.

89 Ace Pilots refers to the Second World War pilots, and specifically to Wing Commander Douglas Bader who remarkably piloted a Spitfire with two prosthetic legs.

90 A Purple Heart is the medal awarded to American military personnel since 1917 who are wounded or killed while on active duty.

91 "You'll get it out in theatre" was the catchphrase of this deployment, which occurred at great scale and pace. As one of the first 'out in theatre', to set up the field hospital and prepare for the concentration of troops in Kuwait, I experienced a good deal of friction due to re-supply and unavailable equipment. When the war started, on 20 March, most frictions had been resolved.

92 Post-Traumatic Stress Disorder.

93 A spring-loaded syringe device was issued to every British soldier for use in emergency to counter the effects of nerve agent poisoning. It contained three drugs (atropine, avizafone, pralidoxime), to be injected into the thigh. Combo-Pen could be self-administered, or used by a medic. These agents were highly stable, which did permit extension of the shelf-life.

94 Anxiety was expressed while deployed, by reservists in particular, that after deployment there was no guarantee their job at home would have been protected.

95 'Mum's cake' refers to the fruitcake that my mother would send by post on all my deployments, including 'early entry operations'. Bizarrely, the cake arrived by British Forces Post Office as we were setting up the hospital, and before we received the necessary supply of blood products.

96 The construct in each portacabin bedroom was a mattress on the floor, surrounded by a wall of breeze blocks with a small crawl space to enter, and a steel sheet 'roof' with an additional layer of sandbags. It was widely regarded as a nightly coffin in which to attempt sleep.

97 The passage of hearses through Royal Wootton Bassett is the subject of *The Black Snake*.

98 Royal Air Force (in reference to the colour of the serge uniform).

99 An absence of military medals, which would indicate a lack of prior service in the armed forces.

100 Regret, expressed by Prime Minister Tony Blair who led the country to war, when the evidence to support war was subsequently criticised in the Chilcot Inquiry.

101 Lieutenant Colonel Henry Beecher, a medical officer on the 1944 beach landings at Anzio, Italy, who observed the paradox of the severely injured making little or no noise. He attributed this to the injury being the ticket home and their perceived release from the misery of war.

102 Blighty was the soldiers' nickname for Britain: a 'Blighty' injury was one that was serious enough to warrant being sent home.

103 *Legion*: the Royal British Legion

104 My experience of this event is described in detail within *Belfast Bomb*, which I regard as the origins of my use of poetry to express and move on from serial traumatic experiences.

105 9/11 is the idiomatic reference to terrorist attacks on the Twin Towers in New York on 11 September 2001, which heralded the Global War on Terror.

106 7/7 refers to co-ordinated terrorist attacks in London on 7 July 2005.

107 Military abbreviation for Mass Casualties, indicating that medical resources are overwhelmed.

108 Ferrous pigment refers to the red–brown colour of blood due to the iron in haemoglobin.

109 Dr Elizabeth Ness McBean Ross (1878–1915), one of the first women in Scotland to gain a medical degree, died from typhus in the military hospital in Kragujevac on 14 February 1915. This anniversary is still celebrated in Serbia, when schoolchildren across the country are taught about her courage and bravery.

110 A senior civil servant who led the independent investigation, that reported in May 2022, into alleged rule-breaking parties at 10 Downing Street during the Covid-19 pandemic lockdown.

111 *As-well* replaces the traditional *A-men* at the end of a hymn.

112 'Herald signs' refers to pre-existing common mental disorders including anxiety and depression, or pre-existing Post-Traumatic Stress Disorder (PTSD).

113 'Addiction' refers to gambling (and the associated adverse financial consequences), together with alcohol and substance abuse.

114 An Army term that defines an individual's trade, such as infantry, cavalry, engineer, signaller, gunner or medi

115 This poem has been set to original music by Cate Carter. In the musical arrangement, there is deliberately a wider inclusion of both the individual voice (which becomes gender agnostic) and the responding voices (who are the 'family'). The lyrics of the chorus are adjusted from "*Military wives, Rock of your lives*" to be "*Your family, Your rock in the sea*".